Lose Yourself,

Pursue Jesus

Words of Truth That Will Pierce Your Soul

Donna Robertson

Manufactured in the United States of America

10 9 8 7 6 5 4 3 2 1

Library of Congress Cataloging-in-Publication Data is available.

ISBN: 978-1-63769-308-7

E-ISBN: 978-1-63769-309-4

This book is dedicated to my sister Jennie.
She passed away March 12, 2018, after a thirteen-year
battle with ovarian cancer. She is always loved, never
forgotten, and forever missed.

Proverbs 31:25 (NLT)

*"She is clothed with strength and dignity, and she
laughs without fear of the future."*

Preface

I spoke almost every day with Jennie, and I miss hearing her voice. Furthermore, I miss talking with her about everything under the sun, and I miss laughing those good belly laughs with her. We hardly talked about Jesus because we did not know much about Him. Most of the things I have written in this book are things that I learned after Jennie died. It upset me that I did not know certain things about this world and the Bible until after she was gone. After Jennie passed away, I yearned to come up with something I could do in her memory that would also help other people at the same time. I would pray about it, and then research what other people had done for their deceased sisters. Not only that, but I donated to different causes that she would have loved. She had a big heart and loved to help people too. I scrap booked a photo album from her birth up to the day she passed. I wondered if I would ever get it finished, but I did complete it through a ton of tears. It made me happy to do these things, but they were not that exact thing I was looking for to honor her memory. I had this empty, incomplete void that I could not fill.

I had to give it to God fully and trust that I would hear from Him and know "it" when I saw it. I was in bed one night reading when suddenly deep down inside me there was this voice telling me to write a book in memory of Jennie. It could not be, I must have heard wrong, so I continued to read, but I heard it again. It happened three to four times, this hearing it and continuing to read. I stopped reading and started paying attention and I heard it again. I could not believe this, and I began crying and sweating. But, at the same time, I was excited, and I did not know what to say except, "thank you, I think?" I had to take some time and let it digest. Furthermore, I needed to make sure this was not me thinking some silly thought. I knew that I did not know anything about writing a book, so I prayed and asked for confirmation and I prayed with someone at church. It was not long, and I received multiple confirmations, some from people to whom I had never mentioned anything. I was nervous and was having a lot of different thoughts, but I eventually calmed down. I had to go back to whose idea this was and let Him show me step by step how He wanted me to do this. Not only that, but I had no idea how to make this happen and had it been up to me, it would have never been started.

Journaling has been my way of communicating with the Holy Spirit for the past six years. This is how I hear, stay focused, and let Him guide my life. My journal entries are inspired by everyday occurrences. Whether it comes from my life or someone else's life, I like to look at the ways of this world and our actions, then see what the Bible says about similar situations and occurrences and the journaling begins. Not only that, but I receive life lessons, and then I can share them with others. Furthermore, I am growing closer to God every day and becoming the person He created me to be. I have included journal entries from over the past few years, along with some life lessons I am being shown in my own life. There is some scripture reference with fragments of verses that came to mind when writing this. In this book are things that I would like to have shared and talked about with Jennie. I know we would have had a challenging, but fun time, learning, and growing in who He is, and who He wants us to be. I know there would have been a lot of laughing and crying, but mostly laughing. Until I see her again, this book, I hope and pray, helps someone else to learn and grow into a close relationship with Christ, our Lord and Savior and be set free.

Acknowledgement

The writing of this book would not have ever come to fruition without my family, friends and the life experiences that have strongly impacted my life. My daily journaling started as a way for me to learn how to express myself and to reflect, review, and revisit where I had been, the choices I had made and what I would need to do differently in the future. The writings continued to grow beyond something I could never have planned on my own. I struggled to put the words from a journaling concept in my head, to putting the words on paper to read as a book. My son, Dalton told me to just write, and I did. Even the times when I could not come up with the words to express myself, I just wrote my jumbled words and thoughts and kept writing, and it has been a process to work through. This began at one of the most difficult times in my life, but it allowed me to focus on something good and not the questions and confusion I was facing. I have waded through a lot of emotions on this journey, and I realize how much I need Jesus as He carries me through this life with His steadfast presence.

Table of Contents

In the Wilderness

I have hung out in the wrong places for most of my life. I have experienced cheating, lying, abuse, and emotional instabilities. I began hanging out in bars when I was too young to be there, and it was awkward at first, and I felt out of place. Not only that, but I remember going down the steps thinking *I should not be here*, but I ignored that thought and went in. Do not misunderstand me, this was not the first time I had a drink, it was the first time I drank in a bar. I did not think it was a big deal, I was with some older friends that I had known for a while, and they went all the time.

Everyone was nice, laid back, having a good time and after a while, I began to relax. I wanted to fit in with them and be accepted. It was worth it to me to go there and be out of my comfort zone if that was what I had to do to fit in with them. I've never been a popular person or part of any one group. Maybe this was just what I needed in my life to feel complete and understand who I am, why I am here, and what I am supposed to be doing.

I grew up in Southern Illinois with my dad, mom, and three sisters. We lived a quiet, comfortable life. In fact, it was quite a good life in a lot of ways. My dad worked and my mom was able to stay home with the four of us girls. We had a nice, comfortable home, we never went hungry, we had clean water to drink and wash with, and we had clothing. We had extended family we would spend time with throughout the years and on the holidays. I went to school and had friends and did school activities. We had storms in our life just like everyone else. I fought with my siblings and got mad at my parents for not letting me go out. As I got older, I would get into trouble a lot because I had a rebellious spirit inside me and I would not listen. It was a typical childhood from my perspective. But as I grew up, I also hoped that there would be more-more to this existence than just being "fine" than just being "okay." At that time, I did not know my life was empty and lonely. I would get discouraged for no reason and would turn to drinking, trying to find happiness, myself, and real meaning in this world.

I do not ever remember praying, discussing or even really thinking about who Jesus is, or want to know why He willingly gave up His life. I was not raised in church, and it was not a topic in our home. There was no concern on my part for me, at that time to want to know anything about Jesus, or about having a relationship with Him. Although, I do remember going to vacation Bible school once, and I remember having to memorize a short verse, *The Lord is my Shepherd, I shall not want*. It made me nervous, and I was scared I would not remember the words to say when I was called for my turn. I did not want to mess it up and look dumb in front of everyone. I remember feeling a lot of pressure on myself to do good, and not make a mistake. That handwritten verse is still clear to see inside the front part of my black Bible. Also, I remember my grandma telling me to read Proverbs. I cannot recall the conversation we were having as to why she would have told me to read it, but these two things are what I remember being introduced into my life about Jesus.

Even as a young adult, getting married, having a son at a young age, and going through difficult times, I never once had the thought to go to church. I may have prayed a little, but God was not my first choice of whom to go to if I needed help. I had to be completely desperate and emotionally exhausted to even consider Him to be a last option in my life for help. If I even considered Him, because He was not a thought, nor was there room for Him in our lifestyle. It was in my mid-forties before I recognized God in my life and started getting to know myself and take ownership for my own issues. Jesus loves us the way we are, but He also wants us to grow and take responsibility for our choices.

On February 15, 2015, I gave my life to Christ. I did not completely understand what that meant at the time. I had been going to a small church in town for about six months. That was a very unproductive and unfulfilled time in my life. Most of what I was experiencing at that time were results of living a disobedient life, and I had come to the end of myself. I desperately needed a new beginning and going to church was refreshing. It was a place where I could laugh, cry, and be filled on the inside. Baptisms were done every month and I watched people over and over accept Jesus Christ as their Lord and Savior every month. I had thought about it, but the thought of me confessing that Jesus is Lord of my life made me nervous. Also, the thought of me getting up on stage to be baptized in front of all those people made me extremely uncomfortable. Why couldn't I just go in there with the pastor and another witness and be done with it? I was getting all these thoughts and excuses in my head like we will do when we are not in our comfort zone. When church was over one morning, I signed up for the next meeting just to see what steps were involved in moving forward.

At the meeting they shared about Jesus and why people wanted to be saved. We did not have to talk, just listen, and I was glad because I was still not for sure about this, and I just wanted to get some information. I felt like it was a good decision for me to be there. The Pastor was talking as he started handing out a piece of paper to each one of us. He wanted us to write down why we wanted to be saved. *Dang, I did not know I was going to have to participate in this meeting.* I just wanted to get some information, I felt like I was in over my head because I had no idea why I wanted to be saved. It seemed like a good idea the week before, but then I was having doubts. I did not communicate myself well to others and my writing was even worse. I struggle to figure out how I am feeling within myself, then he wanted me to share my feelings with him on paper. I wanted to take the paper with me to think and google. I was so nervous I could not remember any of the reasons he had talked about why people got saved. I definitely did not want to draw any attention to myself by getting up to ask if I could leave and bring my paper back to him. My mind was racing, I was sweating and needed to calm down. Thank goodness I had a light sweater on over my blouse because my armpits were sweating profusely. I tried to stay calm and concentrate, smiling and nodding my head, like I understood and knew exactly what I wanted to say. I had to concentrate, but I was feeling so pressured that I could not think straight. On top of all that pressure, I was listening to everyone else's pencil clicking along the wood table, as I just sat there. I had to clear my head and focus. *Donna, why are you doing this? Just write it down no matter how silly, ridiculous or whatever it may sound like to anybody else. These are your thoughts and reasons, nobody else's but mine. So, why am I here? Why do I want to be saved?* My hand started writing, well I should say scribbling, I have the worst handwriting. I just wrote what I knew, and it was that I could not do this alone. I did not know how to do this life. All my life I had been trying to do it on my own, and I had made horrible decisions. I needed someone else to run my life because I could not do it, I had come to the end of myself. There was a little more, but that was the gist of it. To say the least it was not one whole page, but I got my point across about why I was there, and it was very short, and simple.

We always think we need this big dramatic state-
ment to look impressive to others, but I just thought,
I am not concerned with what they think, I need help
and I cannot do this alone. Here it is, and no matter
how impressive everyone else's paper is, I was writing exactly what I had in me, which was not much at
that time. The pastor collected our papers so he could
read them later. We were moving onto the next step
of the meeting, and I felt like this was all going so fast
for me because I still needed a minute to recover from
that first step. While he was telling us that we would be
baptized at the end of the next Sunday's service, I was
wondering what he was going to do with those papers
after he read them. Do we get them back for memora-
bilia? I was thankful we did not have to stand up and
read what we wrote to everyone, or that he did not read
them out loud at the meeting. I would have been more
than happy to hear someone else's reason for wanting
to get saved had he read it, I just did not want mine to
be read, because it was not "spectacular enough" to be
read in front of people. "What would they think of me?"
What a relief this meeting was almost over. Now, I
would have to wait to go through the baptism. We were
told what to wear as we walked through the church, and
he explained everything, which was very comforting to
all of us. I was starting to realize I was not the only one
there who was nervous... I started thinking about how
I did not want to be the first one baptized. Even though

I had seen people do it several times already, I did not want to go first. But I would do whatever they told me, and if I messed up, it would not be the first mistake I had ever made in my life.

Well, next Sunday came and there was no backing out. Thank goodness I had on black and would be getting into water because my armpits were saturated again. I did not get picked first, which in my mind was my first answered prayer. I was probably eighth in line, and it moved quickly. My sister, Sherri and my friend, Steve were there to support me, but I could not think about all the people that sat out in those chairs. I needed to stay focused on breathing, walking to the water, getting down those steps and repeat what the pastor said. Furthermore, I had to stay calm, or I would not be able to speak. Then it was my turn, and I walked to the water, got down the steps, and focused on listening to him, so I could repeat what he said perfectly, be baptized and get out gracefully. I was sitting there on the step, listening as the pastor talked, and I heard him say, "Donna's paper really caught my attention." My heart stopped. Unbelievable, the one thing I did not want to happen, happened. I did not want any unnecessary attention drawn to me. I should have met with him and explained to him how nervous I was about being baptized and getting up in front of everybody. Not only that, but I never would have imagined my paper that said "I could not do this life anymore, and that I needed someone else to make decisions for me" would be the one that got his attention. All the others that immediately knew what they wanted to say, and I was sure they had a lot longer and harder words on their paper than mine. I just could not make sense of how that simple little paragraph could catch that pastor's attention. Well, that was all it took, and the ugly cry was on, and there was no turning it off. That baptism was completely out of my control and not how I had planned or pictured it in my head of how all that would look to everyone. It felt like my mouth was wide open and all my teeth were sticking out. I knew my voice was shaking as I repeated what the pastor said. That was a very vulnerable and humbling experience for me, but I got through it, and I was baptized.

We are not going to get out of what God wants us to do, He is in the business of finding lost people, and He brings them to a new beginning. He met me where I was and brought me through. I was scared and that was not an easy experience for me to go through that day. I am thankful for that experience, and it was part of my new beginning. Not only that, but I needed to be exposed and be an example, that it is okay to be vulnerable in front of people, no matter how hard it is to go through some things, and no matter what people think.

We all get called to do things that are not comfortable and challenge us, but we only fail if we do not try. These challenges are our opportunities to advance in ourselves. When you are facing something in your life that is not comfortable or seems impossible for you, take one step at a time, and do not worry about what people think, you just might be the example God is working through for somebody else's benefit. Jesus loves us, He is a good Father, and He is for us. Doors have opened for me that I, nor anyone else, could have opened, and there have also been some doors closed that I was not able to close myself. He is with me always, even when I did not know who He was; He was with me, and He is with you too. No matter how lost or low down we think we are, we can rise again. He is waiting for you to receive Him and say, *I cannot do this alone, I need you, I cannot do this life without you. I need you to run this life because I do not know how.*

None of us realizes the full potential that we have inside ourselves and that there is a plan for each of us that includes progress and success. So many live depressed and feel defeated when they do not have to. We get impatient waiting and think God does not move quickly enough. It may seem this wait is adding even more pain and problems, so we continue to hold onto our issues thinking we can do it better than He can. It is hard to let go, and let God work in our life so that He can become the foundation that we can depend on. Likewise, it is very hard for people to admit when they cannot do something. We live in a very judgmental world, and it affects our mind. I must consciously, make the effort every day to capture my negative and rebellious thoughts, and teach them to obey Christ.

Jesus never judges us, He created us and there is nothing we can do or say that will surprise Him. He made us all with weakness, so we will all recognize that we need a savior, and it is not ourselves. Being too proud keeps us from letting Jesus into our hearts. We do not get to know all He has to offer, and it keeps us from knowing who He is. We must be willing to go through some difficult times without complaining about every little thing that does not go our way. When we stretch ourselves in this way, we grow and learn the truths about who He is, and who He wants us to become.

I remember a couple of years ago I was reading the Bible, and the Lord had revealed a couple of things to me at that time. I was thankful that I was growing in my relationship, getting to know who Jesus is, and learning about His life and the life He wants me to have. Suddenly, I got so mad, and started wondering why someone never talked to me about Jesus. Why didn't someone take me to church? Why wasn't Jesus, who makes me so happy, not brought into my life sooner? Did I have to emotionally fall apart to see I needed to make some changes in my life? I wanted to call people and demand answers, and immediately blame others for things that are my own problems. This was nobody else's fault, and nobody can change anybody else. I had to stop focusing on the things I thought people did wrong and think of things they did right. Instead of me trying to change people, I needed to work on myself by changing my attitude; the frustrations, selfishness, stubbornness, and being judgmental and unforgiving.

This was not something that I would be able to figure out on my own. For right then, I would accept myself as I was, and believe and trust in the Lord as I followed Him faithfully, knowing that I would not always remain that same way. Day by day I will become the person He wants me to be and fulfill His will for my life. I had to be quiet and listen, so He could show me the roots of my problems. This was not something that just happens automatically, this was going to take a lot of time, and it will be a life-long journey. Would I be mentally strong enough to handle what was being asked of me and let Him show me that I am not the one in the driver's seat?

Jeremiah 29:11-13 (NLT)

"For I know the plans I have for you, says the Lord. They are plans for good and not for disaster, to give you a future and a hope. In those days when you pray, I will listen. If you look for me wholeheartedly, you will find me."

Stepping Out

When we are young and immature, we all do things we regret. We look back and laugh at ourselves and get embarrassed by our actions. Until the veil came off, I was not aware of all the ignorant things I had done. I see it now, and the only words I can come up with are that I wish somebody would have stopped me. Here I am again, trying to blame this on somebody else. I take full responsibility for all my actions, and it is freeing to own my ugly and give it to God. The Lord had to show me how to work through things without beating myself up for being ignorant.

In my reading, I came across these words: conviction and condemnation. It took me a while to keep them straight, but it finally clicked. I am a slow learner, so it takes a minute for things to sink into this brain of mine. I am thankful, I have a patient teacher who understands, that I need to have a huge sign to understand, and then I will still ask if it is my sign or not. Anyway, back to conviction and condemnation. Conviction is from Jesus; He convicts us and shows us areas where we need to make some adjustments. A situation may be used from your life to help open your eyes to something you never realized you are doing, and it helps you to change an attitude or behavior. The lesson lifts us up, so we will learn and be better, not to make us feel resentful for being corrected. The devil condemns and wants us to never forgive ourselves and keep beating ourselves up. Condemnation keeps us oppressed and thinking how terrible we have been.

Pride was the first thing that was brought to my attention. When I first began to realize all the pride I had in my life, I felt ashamed and awful for how I had been acting. I would not let it go and forgive myself. Prideful ways are not easy to overcome when this is what you have known your whole life.

I did not know how I was going to be forgiven or forgive myself. What I did know was that I would have to face this to make the necessary changes in other areas of my life. I did a lot of praying and I asked to see all the areas that needed improvement. I needed to see how I have acted and what I had shown to people about myself. This was frightening, but I needed to know everything about myself if I wanted to start being the person I was intended to be. I wanted to be freed of myself and lighten the load I had been carrying around for years. If this relationship is going to move forward, I would have to be open and honest with myself about my past, present and future. I knew that I was going to see things that would make me cringe and not want to keep moving forward. I was going to keep going no matter how degrading it was. Furthermore, I wanted to improve myself and apply these new principals to my life.

It has taken a lifetime for me to get here and re-alize some things about myself. These growing pains were tough to go through. I hated what I saw, but I also looked to the positive side of being aware of my past actions and knowing how to respond differently when pride starts to arise inside me. I can appreciate that small voice that tells me that I am about to do or say something I will regret later, and I am able to walk away. This flesh tries to overpower me, but I am im-proving.

Life is not good when we are always being put down, belittled, and judged. This is not the kind of life we are meant to be living. We should be trying to become more like Him every day, enjoying this journey we are on. I have a lot of things I need to work on and adjust, and I can get overwhelmed at times because I want these changes to happen quickly and that is not how it works. When condemnation comes, I am reminded of who my faith is in, and I can walk away from the criticism.

It is not our plan or intention to act in ways that are unloving or to say mean things, but we all do it on occasion. I never want to, on purpose, hurt, disrespect, or think I know the best for somebody else. There are things I have said or done meaning well, and I knew my heart was in the right place, but some things are just none of my business. I have learned that what works in my life may not work in everyone else's life. This mouth of mine has needed to be dealt with and taught how to stay shut. A lady I worked with told me something she does is to think of the teeth as a fence that guards the tongue, so it does not lash out and speak when it should not. I like easy concepts like this to help me remember, especially, since this is an area that I continually practice every day. If somebody does not ask for my opinion, I do not need to take it upon myself to tell them what I think or talk about something I know nothing about.

It is not easy to change our ways and not give in to our own desires. When we release the need to be in control of doing things our own way, "my plan, my timing, I deserve the credit, my social status, my way is the only way." The pride can be destroyed, and our relationships will improve.

We live by example and are trained and coached from the time we entered this world, and it will require us making a daily effort to apply undoing behaviors that we want to change. Our personality is who we are and this is what people see about us. They learn who we are, our likes, dislikes and how we act in social settings. Since this is who we have been our whole life, there are some learned behaviors with deep roots inside us. As mine are being uprooted and examined, I am seeing roots in myself I was not even aware existed. I am learning about my strengths and weaknesses and paying attention to both areas and the corrections that I need to make in positive and healthy ways. Likewise, I am learning to be still and simply listen for the revelation and direction I need to keep moving forward in my life.

This is a noisy world we are living in today, and sometimes it seems as though we are drowning in the noise and there is not a quiet spot to be found in all the chaos. I assumed and accepted for a long time that this is just how it is and went along with it, blocking out what I could. When I finally rose above the noise and started to recognize things about myself, things became clearer. I do not have to be who I have always been, do what I have always done and furthermore, I do not have to carry some of the things I had carried with me my whole life.

When I started making these changes it was uncomfortable for me and for the surrounding people. They did not understand why I was making different choices, and I did not understand this process either and would have confused them even more trying to explain it. The best part about changing for me was that for the first time in my life I did not feel obligated to make sure everyone understood the changes that were happening to me. People are always going to have their opinions or assume things they know nothing about in someone else's life. I cannot explain to someone else what is happening in my life to change their perspective, and I have become used to feeling like I do not belong. Not every person is going to like me or things I do, and it is all right. Even though there are improvements in myself, there is still a lot of growing and changing ahead of me.

As I continue this journey, I see why I do not want to go along with the ways of this world, and I am not going to add to the chaos with strife and bitterness. I want the truth about this world, no matter how bad it hurts or what is going to be asked of me, so I can know His ways. Here again, I am not sure what I am asking, or where I am going with all of this, but I need to see things through His eyes, not mine. I want my behavior to agree with Him and live the life He died for me to have, and I want my mind to be healed and whole, whatever that means.

I bought myself an amplified Bible knowing that it was going to take all the in-depth explaining I could get my hands on. I kept challenging myself to stay committed in the Word even though I did not understand all that I read, I persevered and kept reading and believing that it was going to start making sense to me one day. It was overwhelming, and I went to the back of the book and started with the dictionary concordance. I looked up words and scriptures like I was studying for a test and I wrote them out in my journal, it was relaxing for me, I enjoyed it, and it was the small beginning that I needed.

I was blessed with a job where my responsibility was to answer the phone, and with this being my only responsibility most of the time, I could read if I wanted too, so I was able to read and journal almost every day. Also, there was a television in our lobby, and I would watch the different pastors that aired throughout the day and a few of the pastors caught my attention. I started taking notes on their sermons and studying things a little after work and this helped me to understand some things better. In the amplified Bible that I have, there are highlighted areas in each book that explain what some scriptures mean, and these helped me a lot because the book was overwhelming and hard to comprehend. I would read these highlighted areas and go to the scriptures they were referring to, and I started understanding a little more all the time. I was really getting into reading my Bible and listening to some of these pastors on television. Furthermore, I started to DVR them at home to watch at night without work distractions during the programs.

All of this was bringing new life to me. It was hard to describe the new things that were taking place in my life, but I knew something was happening, I was changing, and I liked it. I worked with two ladies that had studied the Bible for over twenty years and I asked them a lot of questions and they each shared some of the things they had been shown in their lives. I would listen and learn, taking from it what I would be able to use in whatever way I was shown. All these happenings in my life have been the Lord driving me to Him, guiding and directing my every turn.

I am thankful for the job that placed me right in front of the Teacher, so I was able to start receiving from Him. It was not a job I would have chosen for myself for a lot of my own reasons, but mainly pride being the number one reason. And, God had a different road for me, not a less, rocky road but a different rocky road. I am still going to face hardships and joy, success, and challenges but through it all God will be at my side, guiding, encouraging, comforting, and caring for me on His road, the right road. I worked at that job for three years, He knew exactly where to place me, so I would start seeing, listening, and learning. Not only that, but I am learning to be available to Him, so He will work in my life and show me the way and the truth of this life.

It was so amazing to me when certain scriptures started jumping out at me, or I would hear something and would have to write it down. All of this was so unlike me and I have had a lot of doubt. I have struggled with knowing how to hear from God. I was not able to discern if something was Him or just me thinking things. It takes focus in this area, but it is beginning to become clearer. I remember to look and see what the Bible says and when my thoughts are in alignment with His then I know it came from Him and not my own thinking. I love when He confirms His Word to me. This has been a very, slow, process, but I am growing in the Word. I know there are always going to be challenges along the way. I remember who has brought me to this point of where I am right now. Not only that, but I would have given in a long time before now, but the Lord is giving me the strength I need to keep moving forward. When I start to feel proud because I have some spiritual growth, I want to be reminded of how I got here and be kept humble. Temptations are in our face every day, and I know who I was, and I know the person I would be right now except for His grace on my life. I give Him all the glory for the progress that has been made in me, and I am in awe of the things that have been shown to me, much that is indescribable and cannot be put into words. I do not see me ever getting bored on this journey with the Lord.

Proverbs 16:18 (NLT)

"Pride goes before destruction, and haughtiness before a fall."

Finding Myself

I have always been around people that had a good idea of what they wanted to do when they got older. Some had already started careers or had goals set for what they wanted to do. I did not have a vision, or even a sense of purpose for my existence. I did not understand my purpose, direction, boundaries, or any limitations. Without them, I did not know what to pursue and follow. It has been disturbing and frustrating for me to not know where I belong and not know where to start to try and figure it out. I never had a desire to be in a certain profession and the one consistent thing I have done throughout my whole life has been reading books, a hobby that I love.

As the years moved along, I always felt less than because everyone around me seemed to have locked into their profession, while I wandered around aimlessly from one thing to another. It was not so bad when I was in high school because I still lived at home and had a routine of school, homework, activities, and a job. My time was filled for that season of my life but post high school my head was empty of ideas. No dreams, desires, I was just living, working, and surviving day by day. I thought I was happy but somewhere down deep in me, I kept hearing "there is more than this." I did not really think too much about it other than, *somebody better show me because I do not know how to discover it.* Especially when you are busy trying to survive from being broke all the time. It seems like there is no possible way to get ahead, to take the time and figure out what is your calling in this fast-paced life. I ignored that inner voice and kept up my same old routine.

I like to care for people, and I thought I would like to be a nurse. I did attend college for a couple of years and I enjoyed college more than I expected. Parents who work full time and go to school with families have a demanding load to juggle and for me something had to give. I finished the semester with intentions of going back but that did not happen. Despite my lack of a degree, I have never had any trouble getting a job. In my varied work history, I have learned how to work with a diverse group of people and adjust to different personalities and situations. One thing I have always loved about switching from different jobs was the diverse people. Throughout all the jobs, I always had the hope that I would find my career niche.

We get blinded by what and how much we think we know. Before my relationship with Jesus, I did not understand that I cannot force anything to work just because I want it to work. All I have ever known is to work and do, and I did not know how or what to ask for from the Lord. I did not know how to give things to God, that did not even make sense to me. I was not aware that there is a part I am supposed to do and then God does the rest. All I have ever known is what has been shown to me about how this world operates.

I had been at a job for about five and a half years, they were going through a structure change, and I was one of the employees not being kept. I went to an employment company and worked temporary jobs through them until I found something permanent. My temporary employment lasted only a few months, and I was offered a position to work full time at an accounting firm. I went into it from the beginning with the wrong mindset. Instead of being appreciative of the opportunity and the new things I was going to learn, I went into it as a careerist just looking for recognition. Undeserving, I was given a high position with great pay. I would have done a better job had I been a better listener and done the things that were asked of me instead of insisting things be done my way. My boss was the mature, responsible one, wanting to start me out slow and make sure this was right for everyone. I pushed and insisted and forced things to be my way hastily, immaturely, and irresponsibly.

I was there a little over a year and that is where things really started to change for me personally. I kept trying to be happy with this job and I did not want to let anybody down because of how insistent I had been in the beginning. Not only that, but I really liked who I worked with, and liked the job. Mentally and emotionally, I was incapable at that time to fulfill the responsibilities of that position. I had to recognize and admit my mistake that I should have started out more slowly. My intentions were genuine, and I did the best I could for the most part.

Something was going on, but I could not figure it out. I did not know God had shown up with His mercy to work in my life. I did not recognize I was at a crossroad in my life and that my response at this time was going to determine whether I fully carry out what He has planned for me. As the pressure was mounting, it was becoming clear that I needed to be broken down of being so strong-willed and prideful, and in order to get my attention, it had to be dramatic. God would have to let me see that I am worthy to be used by Him, but I will have to respond by letting Him refine me, put me through the fire and test me. I needed inward strength and character to withstand the adverse pressure when it comes to complete what He has for me.

I was worried about what people would think. Why was I leaving such a great position? It was a fight I would not win no matter how much I tried to talk myself out of it. I lingered over it a few more months, I took a vacation thinking that might help but the day I returned to work I resigned. It did not feel right to quit, but I knew it had to be done. I was confused and did not understand why I was so adamant about leaving this job. As the words were coming out of my mouth, I did not feel like it was me even speaking. I left there feeling relieved yet confused and lost. I had been so busy ignoring God and not wanting to listen to Him in my life but this was the time for me to listen, pay attention and respond.

Even as I questioned my decisions for a long period after I had quit that job, I would always get a confirmation in some form that this was Him working in my life. Sometimes, we need to be physically removed from the everyday distractions that we have in our lives, then when we are put in the right place and position He can start showing us the defects we have, so we can be freed of them. We all have flaws that we never do anything about unless we are forced too. If we can keep them hidden or pushed down inside us, then we will not have to deal with them, and we can do this for years depending on the circumstances. Then suddenly, for whatever reason you are put in a place where you begin to feel the burn of whom you have become. The time has come, you cannot hide it any longer, and you must face things about yourself that you do not want to face. Lord, I need you to give me the strength and courage to do what you are calling me to do and to help me do it right.

I had been home a few months, and I was starting to look at the jobs that were open. I called the employment agency again to work temporary jobs until I decided what I was going to be when I grew up. This is how the Christian television job came to me. It just kept popping up, and I kept ignoring it, for weeks. I never thought a thing about it as it kept popping up, and I just kept looking over it and thinking, *I wish they would fill that position.* I could not take it because the money was not sufficient, nor would I be comfortable working at a Christian television station. What if I said the wrong thing or cussed? What would people think of me, working at that place? Deep down I did not feel that I would measure up to the people there, and I was very intimidated by that job.

The Christian television job was jumping off the page at me every time I job searched. Finally, I told myself that if that job is still there the next week when I was looking, I would apply for it and just see what happens. I just knew for sure they would never hire someone like me. Well, I worked there for three years and I know for sure that God put me there in that atmosphere. I explained earlier how I got to read, journal, and watch the sermons on television. It was all part of His plan, so I would get to know Him and to know who I am in Him. God can put us on a road, and we do not even realize we are not the one driving.

Instability in our lives brings doubt in our decision- making and makes us think and believe we are less than. I know how that feels to think and believe I am not qualified or good enough. Not having a strong foundation in our life feels like we are always sinking. Let God be your confirmation that even though we may not fit into this world's qualifying ways, we do fit into His. Let Him show you who you are in Him.

Reading the Bible and praying were the first two things that helped me develop a relationship with Jesus. I needed to understand His ways, so I was able to apply them to my life. Like all relationships this requires spending time with Him reading, singing, and listening. Treat it as a true friendship and talk to Him as a best friend and listen to the advice He gives. He will provide answers through our everyday circumstances as we pray, study, and have patience, God will reveal His plan to us. As we begin to understand who we are individually and know who to believe in, all the pressures to prove anything to anyone slowly fades away. If someone had told me six years ago that I was going to experience a complete life change and write a book, I would have said, "obviously, you do not know who I am." But here I am studying the Bible, digging into scriptures, and spending time praying. He is performing impossibilities in my life that I never would have thought possible. He is showing me that I do not have to settle for mediocre. I do not have to be discouraged about any weakness I have or what I am not. These things are not who I am, my identity is in Christ. I will get the results I am looking for in every area of my life by doing things at His Word.

Someone who really knows who they are and what they believe will not think they have to prove anything to anyone. This world is so fortune and fame focused that we do not want to spend a lot of our valuable time trying to get to know Jesus. It takes a lot of time to study and learn meanings of scriptures, but when you give Him your life and let Him complete you, He fills your emptiness with His goodness and His will becomes the focus of your life.

It is overwhelming when I think about what Jesus did for me and you on the cross. The underserved and unearned favor He provides us is hard to accept as His gift to us. Before I believed in Christ, my nature was sinful, I disobeyed, rebelled, and ignored God. Even at my best, I did not love Him with all my heart, but He loved me anyway and never gave up on me. I have a more relaxed, loving nature about myself now. He gives me the confidence I need to stand before all the mountains I need to climb no matter how tall and intimidating they may appear. Not only am I being informed with His knowledge and wisdom, but I see the transformation in and around my life. I have purpose, direction, a better attitude, and healthier behaviors. God gives me the specific things He wants me to have in my life, so I can face this life with confidence.

Isaiah 30:15 (NLT)

"This is what the Sovereign Lord, the Holy One of Israel, says: "Only in returning to me and resting in me will you be saved. In quietness and confidence is your strength. But you would have none of it."

Faith

I did not have a lot of faith in anything before God interrupted my life. Even with God we must build that trust. I did not know if I believed He was going to work things out for good in my life, but I am a risk-taker, so I decided to take Him up on his offer. I have never physically seen or touched Him, but I believe the Holy Spirit is here. No matter how uncomfortable I get, I am going to stick with this and let Him take me through this process for my life.

If you like adventure, action packed and sitting on the edge of your seat, read the Bible. When I consider the things that I have read in the Bible, I am amazed by what the people experienced and the faith they continuously maintained through it all. There were not any of the comforts and ease of doing and getting things like we have now with our fast technology. Comfortable is not a word that I would use to describe life with Jesus then or now. I guess that is why we are continually put in situations to practice using our faith. Our faith needs to be strong because sometimes it is the only thing we are going to have in this life. No matter how much cushion and comfort you think you may have here, real comfort comes when you can hold everything and everyone with open hands, knowing and believing that even through all the suffering we face, this will all work out for good. This kind of following requires big faith with little or no comfort. It is all a part of the refinement process that sets us apart to serve where we are called.

I am completely uncomfortable writing this book and I have a lot of fear. Fear of what God may require me to do with it, fear of failure, fear of rejection, fear of criticism. I journal daily, but those journal entries are for my eyes only, unless I choose to share something with someone. I do have a specific purpose in mind for this book, but my thinking and ways are not the same as the Lord's ways. Is it part of my healing? Will I give it to someone to bless them? Is it going to sit in a drawer until I die, and someone will find it? Is it going to be published? What will people think? It is just these crazy, mixed emotions and feelings. I do not even know how to write a letter without googling an example, much less write a book, so I know this is God working through me and having me do this. As I have said before, I need huge signs, and He has confirmed this to me, several times, so I am going to obey and complete my assignment.

I am learning that faith is stepping out into the unknown, and I am going to make mistakes and I will live through those like I did the other mistakes. We do not know what is going to work for us unless we step out and try different things. No matter what anybody thinks or says, I have faith that there is a purpose for this book, or I would not be writing it and I trust Him. He will work His assignments through any one of us that will become available to fulfill His purposes.

We never know what is going to happen from day to day. We can hope and pray for a problem-free life but that is never going to happen. I am no different from anyone else in this world. I have good times and bad times in my life, worries and scares. Nobody wants their family unprotected and have to face all the trials and tribulations that go on in this world, but we know that is not possible. It is such an empty, helpless feeling to have someone you love so much go through a horrible experience that you have no control over. It is one thing to read about God's faithfulness, but we also need to experience it in our personal life. Each time we trust the Lord during a trial, we know our faith is growing. I am learning how to have faith in the Lord and that He is in control. As I have said, I was baptized in February 2015, and I was not even completely sure what I was doing, but I knew I needed a savior in my life. I remember there being such as desperation in me down so deep that I just could not understand it.

My youngest sister, Jennie, was diagnosed with ovarian cancer in September 2006 she was only twenty-six years old. She had been complaining of a swollen belly for a while and had been to multiple doctors for exams and every time they came up with nothing. Finally, one doctor did find a five-pound tumor inside her. None of us could understand how that could have been missed by so many doctors. I learned ovarian cancer is one of the hardest cancers to detect. It was this diagnosis that started the long road of doctors, chemo, radiation, surgeries, and stints. I remember her first of several surgeries, and it was the longest and hardest wait of our lives. The surgeon came out afterwards to talk to us and tell us what he knew, and it was not good. She was in the last stage of the cancer, and it was really a matter of time. Statistically she would have about five years but since she was young, she would be able to tolerate more. We would have to take it one day at a time. We were all crying; it was horrible and unbelievable.

I will never know how my sister felt or all the thoughts that could have possibly gone through her mind, when they told her the diagnosis. I know the sickening, hopeless indescribable way I felt and all the thoughts I had that were too numerous to count or even keep straight. Personally, I have never gone through something as intense as that and pray I never will. Even though Jennie and I were close, there is no way for me to know what that experience was like for her, and I cannot write about that. But I do know what I went through as her sister and how it affected me.

I look back now and see where I was spiritually and recognize that I needed more of Jesus in my life. But we cannot just cram things into our heads, we must go through some bad things to eventually get to some good things. I am not able to change things from the past, I can just do things differently now and keep moving forward. I stop myself from getting angry because it will not change anything now. We all have times in our life where we wish we would have been able to do some things differently if we knew then what we know now. I would have liked to have been shown some things earlier, so I could have shared them with Jennie, but that is not how it worked out. It seems like a tremendous amount has been revealed to me because I am so spiritually hungry for His Word, but I know it is just a little speck that has been shown to me so far.

Although I had been a Christian, for a couple of years, the comprehension had not come. I was still learning and trying to figure out what all this being saved really meant. What does it mean to have Jesus in my life? Also, there was this voice telling me, that I would never get through this life happy without Jesus in my life. I was done with turning to the wrong things in my life to band-aid problems and relationships, I needed to get over this mountain, but I did not know how to do it. I kept trying to do better, but it never lasted. It was so easy to drink and keep things buried. I remember asking every day that I would get so sick that I would never want to even look at a drink or a cigarette again. I always went back to partying and the temporary fix to not think about reality. There were times that I would be sick for days after going out, and it was just ridiculous. I wanted to stop, but I would let my flesh win every time I felt uncomfortable.

Finally, after years of going out and drinking and six months of this ridiculousness of me getting so physically sick, I was over it. I did not have to fight that bottle anymore. The weight that was literally lifted from me is hard to describe. The best way would be to compare it to the day I was baptized. I thought, if I feel this tremendous over not having the desire to go out and drink, how would I feel if I just let go of everything that keeps me weighted down. Obviously, He was leading me down a good path of making some better decisions and changing some of my old habits. I was curious to see what He was going to do with me, knowing how much I needed these changes in my life. So far, I had let the consequences of my wrong decisions run my life, and I was headed no place but down, so I am going to put my faith in God. I do not know what I am saying except I am ready to get the process started. Up until now I have given a lot of my time and years to sin and had become imprisoned. Now, I will have to dedicate even more of my time and years to work out His plan to set me free. Lord, here is the key, I will go with you anywhere you want to take me.

I always had this voice telling me there is something more than this. No matter where I was in life, happy season, bad season, I just kept hearing it. I never knew what it meant, but now I wanted to know. I am listening so help me Lord, show me what you mean.

As I had said before, I was given the job at the Christian television station and I know it was a gift from the Lord. He let me work there for three years, and I was able to read the Bible and hear Christian broadcasting every day. It was no coincidence; it was a time for me to be examined and find the areas that could potentially discredit me or spoil what God has for me. Not only that, but it was a time to look at my heart and to prepare me for an opportunity to strengthen my foundation so that in the future my life could support what lies ahead for me and all that is going to be entrusted to me. I am learning to embrace the process and be patient in difficult times of waiting for the next step to be given to me. I need to be refined to make sure that I am right and that my foundation is strong, that I will be ready for the next seasons of my life and the long- awaited assignments He will give me. The Lord was doing a work in me that I was going to need and depend on every day of my life.

It is difficult to be so far away from people and not be able to help them the way you want to. We can do our part and let God do the rest. It was a struggle for me to not be with my sister every day and help her. There was tremendous guilt, and I did not know what to do but pray, and really did not even know what or how to pray. I would travel there and see her and the rest of my family as much as possible, probably more than was needed, but I just kept trying to do, do, do, trying to make it better and make myself feel better. None of that changed the situation, I did not know what to do to make this better or fix it, so I poured myself into the Bible. The desperation and fear I felt for Jennie and the whole family was overwhelming at times. I just wanted to be there all I could to help, spend time with my family and try to keep living this life as "normal" as possible.

Just because I want to help people and do things for them does not mean they necessarily want my help. I take it upon myself to step in and start doing something without asking and that can be offensive to people. I have had to take a step back and be careful with my overbearing approach. It may come off as me wanting to take over, or that my way is the right and only way. That is never my intention, and I am listening and more aware of people's reactions when I ask if I can help them. There have been a lot of mistakes and at times, it has taken a lot of practice and restraint for me to stand back. I will continue to make conscious efforts when I am put in these situations and realize that doing nothing may be the best response.

It is hard to have faith in something you cannot see, but the more I use it and rely on it the more I see it in my life. As I read the Bible and had difficulty understanding it, I had faith that one day it was going to start making sense, and it did, after a while. It was so exciting to me the first time I had a revelation and understood something that I had read over and over. It was such an amazing feeling, and I did not waste time questioning why my eyes had been closed so long. I wanted to know more, and I could not wait to see what else would be revealed. It was my new party, and I was having so much fun and I felt fantastic the next morning. The more truth I had, the more stable and stronger I became.

The days, weeks, months, and years went by of watching my sister fight the battle of her life. There are some things in this world we are never going to have an answer for, and I believe all our why's and how comes will be answered one day. I clung to Jesus because I did not know how to go through that without Him. I had to pray and trust Him to help me every second of every day. All day I listened to Him and carried on as Jennie laid in bed day after day so sick. It was unbearable, and He is all I knew to rely on so that those circumstances did not dominate my life.

Something big was happening at that time. My faith was being stretched to the max and my patience was being developed in overtime. All my doubts were being confronted and slowly but surely being conquered. My relationship with God was growing deeper. He knew what lay ahead and was preparing me in advance. I was completely out of my comfort zone. This was a necessary part of the process and I had to stay focused on Him, or it was not going to turn out well. The devil was right there with every temptation you could imagine waiting to destroy my life, but I was not about to let him have his way, I needed to let God be the only God in my life to be able to go through what was headed my way. There was no possible way I would ever be prepared to lose Jennie and I had to let Him carry me down that road.

I never lost hope for Jennie to receive a miracle. The deterioration we all witnessed was unbearable, and I was thankful for the time I had with her. I know now it is not God's intent for us to die young and live sickly lives. He is a good God and wants us to be healthy, whole, and happy. I could sense throughout that whole experience the crossroads I kept coming to in my own life. The decisions and choices I made were so vital at that time in my life. There are not enough words to explain all the different emotions I was having at the same time. It was such a confusing time in my life. I wanted to believe and have faith in Him but did not know why He would not heal my sister. He knew how sick she was. As my relationship has grown in Jesus, I have learned to not ask why. Not that I accept everything that happens, but there are too many variables that I am never going to understand. I am going to have faith that He will work all things out for good. I have had too many times in my life when the Lord has shown up to not keep trusting and having faith. A lot of times when I have had something on my mind and question something in my life and it just so happens that the answer gets put right in front of me. Whether it be through a devotion, a person, or something from nature, He has let me know that His presence is here with me, and He hears me and knows exactly what my needs are and when the time is right to answer.

I had my first physical touch with the Holy Spirit on the day of Jennie's funeral. Leading up to the funeral in the months before she died, all I could say or even think was to trust God and do good. This is all I kept repeating for months and for the Lord to help me do this right. It was an emotional time for me, and I did not want to take out my emotions on another person. I wanted to trust God and do good, So, these were my words, "I'm going to trust God and do good and Lord, help me do this right".

On March 11, 2018, my sister Sherri called me about 8:00 p.m. and told me she and Felecia, my other, younger sister, were at Jennie's house, and that Jennie was not doing well, and they thought I should head that way. Everyone who has experienced the roller coaster ride of cancer faces a lot of times not knowing if this is the time. Jennie had been through so much and so many ups and downs, and because we did not know when the time would come, I tried to spend as much time with her that I could. As I drove to her house, I thought about how she might pass before I got there. I did not want that to happen but if it were to happen, I was going to be okay, She had suffered long enough, and I was not going to selfishly think of myself.

The next day, Jennie passed away. I was still rehearsing the words to trust God and do good in my head and was numb at that point. There were a lot of people starting to come in and out and my mom was not doing well, for obvious reasons. I remember telling my mom the words I had kept repeating to myself because I did not know how to comfort her. Losing my sister crushed my heart and part of me was gone, so there is completely no way for me to understand what it would be like to lose a child. I had to trust God and be good to my family. Having never been involved in planning a funeral, I would have never thought that the first funeral I would help plan would be for my baby sister. This was just not right and unbelievable, but I was thankful that I was able to spend a lot of time with her and had said everything I needed to say to her. She knew I loved her, and I know she loved me.

There are things in the Bible I have learned that I wish I would have known then to share with her, but that was not how it worked out. I have learned how to cope and not be mad at God because He did not show me certain things until after she was gone. I will keep my faith and believe He is going to work this out for good. She had a purpose here, and she made a difference in a lot of people's lives.

When the funeral was over, we were all going back to Felecia's house. I felt the need to go to Jennie's house. I think because we had been in her bedroom now for years talking, laughing, crying, and watching scary movies that I did not like. But being in her room is where I felt so connected to her and I needed to go there right then. We were extremely close, we had our differences, but we also had the type of relationship that we could say and share anything, and neither was offended nor carried grudges. Not only that, but we always picked up right where we left off with no questions. She was not only my sister, but a best friend. She was hilarious and had her unique way of doing things. We loved and accepted each other for whom we each were individually. I laid in her bed and I could finally cry, not that I did not before, but it flowed out and it was good. I stayed for a while, and then I got up, I took a couple of her t-shirts and I left. Jennie's house was a place I knew I would never be able to walk into again. Although, I had gone back one more time, I was not able to stay. When I left Jennie's house, I was supposed to go to Felecia's house but I could not go, I had a five-hour drive home and I knew the drive would be good for me, as that had always been a place where I talked to God, on a good road trip.

It was on this trip home that I experienced a physical touch from the Holy Spirit. I was driving, and I started crying hard and was consumed with emotion. I pulled over on a gravel patch off the side of the road. My face was in my hands as I was crying and trying to get a hold of myself. I felt a brush against my right leg, I jerked my head up, and I was stunned to not see something next to my leg. It overwhelmed me and I had to tell someone about this. I immediately called Felecia and told her what I experienced. I knew she believed me but maybe that was not the best time for her to try to understand what I had experienced. She told me to come over that I should not be driving, but I explained that was really what I needed to do and that I would let her know when I made it home. The whole family was there, and I felt bad for not going, but I also had a strong sense that it was best for me to go home. We hung up, and I knew I was not alone. There are signs of God's, blessings all around us. We do not always pay attention to what is happening right in front of us and try to ignore or brush things off. I did try to brush that off, I was looking to see where my purse was or if something had fallen and hit me but there was nothing around me.

It is always easier to thank God for His blessings during times when all is well, and the sickness is healed. But He blesses us even in the wilderness, He blesses us when we are consumed with grief and sadness and the uncomfortable unknown. He blesses us when things are so difficult that we try to keep moving to change the circumstances. God will not just remove us out of trials and tragedies, He will come alongside us and give us a renewed hope as we journey onward. I had such a peace in the middle of all that overwhelming sadness. He made me smile, and I knew that He was there holding me together because I am in control of nothing.

Faith

Proverbs 3:5-6 (NLT)

"Trust in the Lord with all your heart; do not depend on your own understanding. Seek his will in all you do, and he will show you which path to take."

My New Normal

God's Word has been the best medicine and therapy I have ever been given. He is working on and repairing all my broken pieces. I feed on His Word daily which keeps me spiritually strong. Every decision I make ultimately impacts everyone in my life. I am a Christian who has a strong relationship with Jesus. I can talk about it all day long or read the Bible twenty-four-seven, but if I am not living it and doing what I know His Word says, then it is useless.

There were a lot of dark and depressing days after Jennie died. I had to make a conscious effort every day to stay with God. I prayed for my family multiple times a day, believing, and hoping for the day when the heaviness would be lifted, even a tiny bit. Not only that, but I wanted to believe His Word and let it work in my life, so I persevered daily no matter how hard I would cry, spending time reading, singing, and talking to Him about how I felt, and making it through with His help. Although none of us had much to say I would call my parents and check on them. It is heartbreaking when there is nothing that you can do to comfort someone, but I kept believing that God had them and knew what to do for them.

I had this inner voice telling me to stay in the Word, and do not stop. "No matter how bad it gets trust me,

I am faithful." I knew I had faith; I just could not understand it at that time. I made the decision to believe and stick with it every day. My thoughts kept wanting me to rehearse things I did not understand. I was not going to listen to the confusion that kept popping up. I must do things differently and there were changes to be worked on and if I wanted this new normal to be successful, I had to go all in. There was no better time than the present because I was at the lowest, I could have possibly been.

I went back to work after a couple of weeks, and everyone was kind and gave me a warm welcome back. I handled it well, of course we all have our moments when you just burst out crying after losing a loved one. This new normal was going to require practice and getting used to new thinking, ways, and habits. It helped me to have something positive and good to keep my mind focused on, and I was anxious and excited about a new beginning. I did not know what was in my future, but I knew I was in good hands.

I focused on the Christian programs that I liked, and I kept reading. We had guests that would come on the program and one of the guests talked about spiritual discernment. I had never heard of spiritual discernment. I learned that when we choose to grow in the knowledge of God, we are choosing the best way to live. We should not be living by how we are feeling because our feelings are constantly changing, and we should not just go by what we see, because things are not always what they appear to be. This is where discernment comes into our life and helps us to evaluate a situation and decide what is the best decision for our life. To live in God's will, we must have a discerning spirit. We need to walk in a manner that represents Him well, and we will experience His joy and peace in ourselves.

It has taken me some time to learn and know His ways. I have discovered some situations that I think are right for me, are not, and I will get a strong sense when I need to go another way. We can get overloaded with so much information and a lot of what we think is true, is not. We must be able to distinguish between the two and not accept everything we hear or see.

I was starting to look forward to facing the challenges of the day. It was intimidating and awkward to think like this, but I knew it was the right thing to be doing. It was an interesting challenge for me to learn how to change my thought pattern and to start thinking the way the Bible tells us to think. In the back of my mind, I knew I also wanted to share this knowledge with someone else. This was just too good to keep it all for myself and I wanted other people to know that if I could make drastic changes during one of the hardest times in my life, they could too.

Living this new normal was one of the most challenging things I had ever done. It is not something you can just do on your own. I needed to receive help every day, or it would have been impossible for me to have succeeded. Let me not get enough sleep or be hungry and this mouth would lose control, and then I would be back to square one. Every time I thought I could handle it on my own and walk away from my Helper, I would end up in another wreck. I messed this up all the time by letting things that irritate me, control me. I am never going to be perfect, but I am improving.

I am becoming a better listener and I try not to talk about things I have no clue about. I want my mind to be renewed and think clearly, understanding what I am hearing and have any misconceptions stripped away. For so long I had just gone along with what I was told, I did not realize I could make my own choices even when I was older. We can get so caught up in thinking the way everyone thinks and having the same opinion as the crowd. We either do not want to make anyone mad or just do what we have always done. When we go along with the crowd, before we know it, we completely lose ourselves as individuals.

I am learning to pay attention every day to the things that irritate me. I can either let these irritants ruin my whole day or I can find out what precautions to take the next time it happens. Also, I am learning to detect who and what pushes my buttons, so I do not live in strife and think negatively of others or me. By recognizing and setting new boundaries it has helped me to be my best and has made positive improvements in my quality of life.

I make the choice every day to try and give God my best, I do not fit Him in when I can for a few minutes, He is my priority and all else comes second. Some things are just not right for my life anymore. I go out and have a good time, I just do it differently than I used to. I am in a different season of life, and I am ready to move forward and see what lies ahead. I do not want to offend people or make anyone feel rejected, likewise, I do not want to be made to feel guilty because I choose not to do something. Furthermore, I cannot be successful in this life if I continue to go along with my same old ways. There are always going to be challenges to face in this life for the choices we make. We will never completely know and understand each other's choices, and we are not going to be accepted by everyone we meet. I do my best to have a peaceful life and not let others try and steal it. It will be impossible to enjoy a life of peace if I do not study myself and identify my peace stealers. It might be a good idea for you to keep a list of every time you get upset and ask what about the situation got you upset or caused a problem? Write it down and be honest, or you will never be free. I have seen the benefit of growing closer to God, and it has been greater than the difficulties I have experienced to get here.

Change is good, it is not always easy, but it is good,

and I have found it to be refreshing. I am doing my best to live by His Word. I get impatient and frustrated, but I know that I cannot pressure myself into changing before it is time. My part is to make right choices, have the right thoughts and trust that God will give me the grace to do what I need to do. Sometimes even when we look changed on the outside, or we may "feel" better that does not change who we are on the inside. A person who comes to know Jesus Christ as his personal Savior is changed. I do not want the same things anymore, and I do not want to live the same way anymore, I want to live my new life.

I never used to consider how my thoughts affected me and everyone else around me. I do now because I know that I need to have healthy thinking. Before, I used to say negative things or be in a grouchy mood and speak awful to people. After I started to change my words and attitude, I noticed a big difference all around me, and there was a different kind of energy around me. It was a rough start and I struggled daily, especially on those tired or hungry days, I knew where I messed up, and I had to regroup and start over a bunch of times. Thankfully, we get a new beginning every day and eventually I saw some progress. Again, I will never be perfect, but I am improving and that is what matters.

There have been people, and situations that did not bring pleasure to my life. None of those adversities and sufferings I experienced are going to waste. It is all being used to rebuild me from the ground up. I am being shown how to carry myself, whether it is an attitude, pride, or mood, some of my broken pieces are being restored. After much stubbornness and rebelling I realized it is much easier to submit to the Lord and get through the hard things, so I can move on to something else. If I do not learn how to apply His Word to my life I will not move to the next level. I will continue to be put in those same situations until I learn how to think and adjust my attitude. It is not a comfortable place and I have a "one day at a time" mindset because this journey is for a long term. My short-term goal is to have patience with the journey and make a little progress every day. It is more important that I am growing and learning from my mistakes rather than I live a quiet, comfortable life, never realizing that there was a bigger plan for my life.

Ephesians 6:11-17 (NLT)

"Put on all God's armor so that you will be able to stand firm against all strategies of the devil. For we are not fighting against flesh-and-blood enemies, but against evil rulers and authorities of the unseen world, against mighty powers in this dark world, and against evil spirits in the heavenly places. Therefore, put on every piece of God's armor so you will be able to resist the enemy in the time of evil. Then after the battle you will be standing firm. Stand your

ground, putting on the belt of truth and the body armor of God's righteousness. For shoes, put on the peace that comes from the Good News so that you will be fully prepared. In addition to all of these, hold up the shield of faith to stop the fiery arrows of the devil. Put on salvation as your helmet, and take the sword of the Spirit, which is the word of God."

Heart Problems

Life is more than being physical with touching and seeing, there is a spiritual part as well. Our emotions play an important role in our life and need extra attention to stay healthy. If we do not learn how to manage our emotions and keep them under control, they can potentially take over our whole being. Feelings are powerful and will either lead us toward God's will or away from it. I have had times when I have been stressed and let emotions take over and dominate my thinking. It seems like a relief at the time to get things off our chest, but boy will the regret come later. Embracing my new normal was also going to include me living a life that is free of offense. Every time I ran into something that tempted me to be offended, I would take it like a test and see if I could pass, and I failed for a long time. Finally, I was getting a handle on some things and saw that I was letting these things offend me and disrupt God's plan for my life.

I never knew that I did not have to be mad just because I "felt" mad. I lived this way for a long time with such anxiety in my life. It could change at any moment and from one extreme to another, and my emotions had been out of control and stressed to their maximum point on multiple occasions. It was scary to be out of control like that, and I needed help to grab a hold of these emotions and be stable within myself. I did not realize how much energy I was using and wasting until I started changing. When we are stressed and exhausted emotionally and physically, it leads to bad decisions, and we must guard what we put into our minds, so we do not make foolish decisions and act quickly.

I had to forgive people around me that I did not ever want to forgive. I believed I had the right to be angry and that anger was justified. I did not have the right to withhold forgiveness, regardless of the pain I experienced. There are several instances that come to mind where I had been mad and held grudges internally. This just showed how immature and self-centered we can get when we expect too much out of people.

We may not understand another person's situation, and it is not our plan to let people down, but it does happen. Most of the time we misunderstand each other's circumstances. No matter how bad some of my pain had been, over time I had been able to forgive and let myself be free. The only person we hurt is ourselves when we chose to not forgive. When I was working through some of these things, I saw that I am not the judge and that I could never forgive anyone more than He has already forgiven me.

I try to keep it simple and mind my own business. I need to pay attention to what I am supposed to be doing and not compare myself with what others are doing. I only want what is meant for me and my life. It is not about a title or pay, it is about me doing what is asked of me, in the place I am positioned. I want to live my true life and not emotionally react to every single situation that pops up. Having control over all these different emotions requires discipline. Every day is not as smooth as I would like, but I do see results in my life.

The most challenging obstacle I faced was not only having to submit to the Lord and be baptized, but I needed to submit to my husband. At times, it felt like I was being skinned alive and I had to go into overtime for this one. I had negative thoughts about men and did not want to be bossed around. There had been a few bad relationships and I did not know how to handle them at that time; I was young and immature, I did not know how to communicate and work through problems or walk away. I am not even sure if I ever knew the real meaning of submission until I looked it up. As I look back on my life, I see pride, selfishness, fear, and that I wanted to be in charge, even if it meant disaster, I did not want to listen or take advice. I could not make this challenge easy on myself and just submit; I would have to go through some tests if I wanted to learn how to have peace in this area, because I am the one that is wanting to live this changed life.

Manipulation, domination and trying to control a person is wrong. People do this to each other and for some people it is all they know. Learning the truth about things will change your whole outlook on this life. We must retrain our minds to think the right way and get on the right path that leads to peace and joy. My attitude, the words I say, and how I say them affects the conversations I have. I need to listen to what is being said to me and not get mad because something may not go my way. There are things done a certain way for a certain reason that I may never understand, and it all goes back to me not talking about what I do not know. I have mentioned before that you cannot be successful on this journey without God. It took well over a year of me trying to adjust to this new obedience. I did not mention that I was going to start doing my best to listen better, I did not need any comments or added pressure. This was serious business and I really needed to concentrate if I was going to succeed. I would talk and share my opinions, but I did it differently than I normally would have. I left out a lot of words that I did not use anymore, and I said or made suggestions with a different attitude. After a long while I realized I did not have to be afraid of being controlled or lorded over. I studied about submission and what is right according to the Word. I continue to grow and mature in this area, I trust the Lord that by submitting to Him first, everything else will be taken care of, and I know He has my best interest.

My life is blessed, and I am grateful for that. I also know that I will never have a problem free life. We will all face trials and tribulations in this world. When things seem all wrong, I will trust the Lord and endure. I knew I was changing, and I also started noticing a difference in Bret's attitude, and he was listening and hearing me a little more, nothing major but a little more. I do not expect anyone to understand fully the Lord's way with me, anymore, then I can fully understand His ways with others. We are not perfect, now and then I want to scream when the strife arises, but it reminds me of how easy it is to behave in a fleshly and emotional way. I need to be on guard against the temptation of pride and a bad attitude and think before I react.

John 16:33 (NLT)

"I have told you all this so that you may
have peace in me. Here on earth you will
have many trials and sorrows. But take
heart because I have overcome the world."

Rejection

We forget that we are never alone and the things nobody else notices, God notices. I saw a commercial, and it just keeps coming to my mind. It was a guy driving his younger brother to football practice and when the boy was getting out of the vehicle the older brother told him to work hard on that field so that someday he would be somebody. It was inspiring and positive, but I thought to myself, *he already is somebody*. He is a young boy that is worthy, special, and he already does matter, he does not have to be seen by a big crowd to "be somebody" and then he will be worthy.

I am not very schooled in the ways of social media. I use it, but not a lot and started asking questions about how some things worked and started talking about "likes." I discovered the importance of "likes" to young adults and the lengths that people go to, so they will get a "like." I did not know there are places you get pictures made to look like you are at a ritzy place, so you can post them, and you will get a lot of "likes." Or you can even pay a monthly fee to get "likes" automated from a robot. I guess I am showing my age and ignorance. It is incredibly sad to me that someone would pay a robot for "likes" to make them feel worthy and valuable. I guess the only way I can relate to it is when I went into that bar with older girls, I wanted people to like me. It is a different time in society of how we respond to the culture, but the concept is the same. We all just want to feel accepted, be important and loved by other people.

There are so many hurting people all over this world that feel rejected and unworthy. I used to think and believe that if I had an idea or said something, and people did not agree with me that they were rejecting me and that was not the truth. I did not know or realize that just because someone may not agree with me does not mean they are rejecting me, they just have a different opinion or way. Not only that, but I lived thinking like this for most of my life, and it was a lie.

Contentment with life is not a feeling, it is a decision we need to make. It does not mean we never want to see change or improvement, but it is about being happy, where we are and with the things we have at different stages in our life. We need to keep a good attitude until we are moved onto the next level. We live in a society where everybody wants to be famous, and few people want to be in the back not being noticed. There seems to be this joined agreement that unless we are on stage, have some big title or not multi-millionaires by the time we are twenty-five, we are failures. This is not the way the Lord looks at people. Many people have not taken the time to get to know themselves and understand why we do what we do.

Self-deception is easy to fall into and one of the

hardest things to face. When we are willing to face the truth about ourselves and examine our motives, God will help us to change for the better and put us on the right track with His will for our lives. No matter what our own social or economic situation may seem like, look beyond that, and find your true self. The humility I needed to face in my life has allowed me to recognize that my worth comes from God alone. To be humbled involved me leaning on His power and guidance and not my own independent way or how others viewed me. He wants to lift us up and give us worth and dignity, despite our human shortcomings. Before we can move forward, we usually have some bad habits that we need to overcome.

I would not have written this book if I had listened to all the excuses swimming around in my head. I had to confront all these excuses and look at each one, pray and make sure I am doing the right thing because I did not know anything about writing a book. Over and over, I kept hearing how inadequate, unqualified, uneducated, and unequipped I was to do this. That this was a waste of my time to share with people how the Word of God changed my life, and that I am a nobody, and nobody cares about what I have to say. The enemy wants me to keep my old mindset and not move forward. We do not have to settle for second best in life, but that is exactly what we will get if we continue listening to the reasons of why we cannot or should not do something. I only fail if I do not try, so I am going to persevere through by completing this book and get the results I am looking for.

The greatest treasure we could ever ask for is to be set free. This is exactly what the Word of God has done for me. My heart and mind have been opened to its transforming power, and it has done a work in me. This takes time to break free from bad thinking and habits, but His Word will attack it, and you will begin to see the truth.

The enemy should have taken me out when he had the chance, when I was living wrong and making wrong choices for my life. Because now I have the powerful, Word of God on my side. I have a new energy, new direction, and new way of thinking that the Holy Spirit has given me. When the Holy Spirit works in you like this, you are truly, changed, and nothing can stop God's will for your life.

2 Corinthians 10:4-5 (NLT)

"We use God's mighty weapons, not worldly weapons, to knock down the strongholds of human reasoning and to destroy false arguments. We destroy every proud obstacle that keeps people from knowing God."

Romans 12:2 (NLT)

"Don't copy the behavior and customs of this world, but let God transform you into a new person by changing the way you think.

Then you will learn to know God's will for you, which is good and pleasing and perfect."

God's Kind of Love

Love is not a topic that I would ever choose to spend time reading or getting to know more about. But I kept coming across how love is the one characteristic that identifies Christians as followers of Christ. I realized that since this kept jumping out at me, I needed to look more into this subject. It is another one of my areas that needed some growth and maturity. I did not want to wait any longer for the repairs to begin and was curious and anxious to see what would be shown about myself and improve who I am in this area. In the back of my mind, I wondered what situations I would be placed in for me to grow and move forward. The most important thing I am reminded is to learn and apply these truths to my life, so I advance to the next level. I am reminded often that I am God's child, and He created me for a purpose. Once I started to recognize that I had worth and value, I learned that these two things are rooted into my relationship with God. I was able to see the areas where I had not loved or respected myself and others.

Love is the key to God's plan for every believer. When we do not like ourselves and who we are, it makes us feel unworthy of anything God has to offer to us. Love teaches us to see ourselves as God sees us. We are God's children and we each have our own unique talents and gifts. One is not more important than the other, and He has a special plan for each of us. But He cannot set you on a path to achieving His goals for your life until you recognize your worth and learn to love the person, He created you to be. When we do not love ourselves, we will not love others, and since people are everywhere, we are going to have to learn to get along with them. Learning to get along better with others, has made a major impact on the quality of my life.

Since I have had the opportunity to work in multiple businesses I have been around a lot of diverse people, and it is important for me to be patient and understanding of those differences in people. I look around, and I appreciate and respect the uniqueness and different gifts we each have. I do not have to feel less than or intimidated because I do not have the same qualities that you have, and it is very freeing.

It was not people that changed, that I can look at them differently, it is because my heart was changed, and I am growing in love. I get along better with people; I am more patient and can love someone who is hard to love. There is no challenge if we are alike and agree on everything. When we are in the company of difficult people, we cannot give them the power to make us miserable. Instead of trying to dodge these people, use these times to grow. I have been through a lot of times when I have reached my growth limit for that day, and it was time to walk away. But as we grow, we will be able to endure these difficulties a little longer each time and become less frustrated as we work through these challenges. There are some situations that we do have to get out of because it is such an unhealthy relationship and there is no other option. Most of the time it comes from hardheartedness and pride.

I have had to recognize boundaries with people and decide what is healthy for me, and not allow myself to be led into unnecessary strife and petty argument. I am learning to humble myself and accept when I am wrong and live my best life with people and be happy. This is another way my character is being built and my rough edges are being smoothed out. I know how I am supposed to act when I am around people that are difficult, and some situations are easier than others to act spiritually mature. This has happened at different times in my life with different people whether it be family, friends, or strangers. No person or relationship is perfect but when we learn to choose peace and understand our own boundaries of who we are, we can put a stop to a lot of conflict before it even starts.

Loving people requires sacrifice, patience, give and take. In this life, we are provided daily, different circumstances that we will continually need to keep adjusting to maintain balance. We accommodate when we can if we want to have successful relationships. When we are secure in Christ, we understand our worth and value in Him, and it gives us confidence to be ourselves. When we love ourselves, it makes it easier to love others and for them to love us.

Love requires us to give ourselves away. As we focus on others, we will discover more joy in our own lives. Investing interest in other lives leads to great relationships in every area of our life. Too often we are driven into relationship by exciting feelings of love and passion before we take the time to develop a friendship. When we do take the time to build a friendship by listening and sharing who we are and respecting each other's choices, it makes a love relationship much more, closer and satisfying.

Sometimes we think we are waiting on God, but the truth is that He is waiting on us. He has already done everything it takes for us to have all our needs met. If we want to see His provision and grace activated in our lives, we must believe Him for it. The Lord has literally changed me from the inside out. I think differently and behave differently, and I encourage everyone to develop a personal, intimate relationship with Jesus Christ. As I spend time with the Lord through reading, praying, and just talking to Him, it makes me thankful for what He has done in and through me and I truly, love myself and others in a balanced way.

2 Corinthians 3:18 (NLT)

"So, all of us who have had that veil removed can see and reflect the glory of the

82

Lord. And the Lord-who is the Spirit –
makes us more and more like him as we are
changed into his glorious image."

Unbound

I may not be experiencing the same volume of problems that I see other people facing, but I know what the Lord brought me from, and I remember who I was before He delivered me. This change in me was only possible by the grace of God. He called me to be baptized, so I would be renewed, grow, and become the person He created me to be. We do not realize it as its happening, but we allow this world to trap us. All the problems and stress of this life weigh us down, and we just keep piling it on year after year and carrying it around. No matter what we do or how hard we try, we cannot escape the pain, negative thoughts, and confusion. We do not know this is sin in our life and that we have trapped ourselves in our own prison. The only way to escape this prison is to stop relying on yourself and give everything in your life to God. He will fill the voids, comfort you when nobody else can, give you love and hope. He will show you His will for your life and your journey will begin.

Furthermore, He will give you the strength and courage you need to do what He calls you to do. I have shared several areas where I had let the enemy come in and was able to make me believe his lies. Also, I have shared some things I look for, and I am not so vulnerable, and the enemy cannot get in so easy now to destroy any area of my life unless I let him trick me through sin or disobedience. That is why I must make God my priority by staying in the Word and not letting the things of this world blind me to the truth.

Jesus wants us to pursue Him the way we pursue the things of this world. I do not let any certain talent, ability, or the things I have, define me. These abilities and things are not who I am; I have a new identity and I have been called to serve Him as His representative, spreading knowledge of Him. We exchange our own desires for His, but these values often make little sense to those who do not know Christ.

Maintaining a godly center in the world is difficult, but we can find support and encouragement from other believers, and together we help each other stay focused on the Lord. I do not want anything or anyone in my life that is going to stop me from putting Him first in any area of my life. Every Christian is called to some type of ministry by sharing the gospel through words and conduct. I have struggled with knowing God's will for my life, and I believe I am doing what He is calling me to do at this time in my life. There are places I have not wanted to go that I thought were absolutely, wrong for me, only to discover that it was exactly where I needed to be. We are purposely positioned in places to lead others to Christ.

I am going to humbly follow Jesus and whether my

life has a large or small impact is up to God, not me. Some of the greatest acts of service are done when nobody is looking. The acts get no attention because they are considered so small to society. Smiling or praying for someone can change someone's whole day or life. I never want to forget who allowed me to write this book and who is making me the whole person that I am becoming. I began this spiritual journey feeling unqualified and not knowing what it was going to require; it has been a very humbling experience for me. Confessing sins, asking for mercy, and praying on my knees to God as He has worked in my life. There is a long way to go, but my life is forever changed, God has done a lot of work behind the scenes, before it manifested in my life. As I spend time in Scripture, I increasingly see from God's perspective what my prayers will be focused on, and what He wills rather than on what I want. Through this kind of prayer, my spiritual needs are met, and I can set aside the unknown questions and live in complete trust with the Lord.

When I got saved, I wanted nothing more than to tell people about the changes that had been made in my life. He saved me and intervened in my life with mercy, instead of the judgement I truly deserved. I will never know all the places, people, and situations He spared me from that I did not realize were not good for me. He has given my life a purpose and put a driving desire in me to share the Good News with everyone. We can all be a blessing to someone and concentrate on something higher than just surviving.

Philippians 3:12-14 (NLT)

"I do not mean to say that I have already achieved these things or that I have already reached perfection. But I press on to possess that perfection for which Christ Jesus first possessed me. No, dear brothers and sisters, I have not achieved it, but I focus on this one thing: forgetting the past and looking forward to what lies ahead, I press on to reach the end of the race and receive the heavenly prize for which God, through Christ Jesus, is calling us."

Afterword

I want to help people who are in the dark by showing the light of the Word to those who do not know what a difference Jesus can make in a person's life. This book is a light for you. I hope after reading it, you will be inspired to learn more about the life that Jesus has for you. He is our main source for everything we will ever need. You can trust Him to show you the truth about your whole life in every area. He will give you courage and compassion, comfort and joy, wisdom, and words throughout your journey, and you may be called to share your journey with others. Sharing about Jesus is our calling as believers, but that does not mean it is always easy. Trust the Lord with the gifts He has given you and represent Him well.

If you would like to receive Jesus Christ into your heart and let Him, be Lord of your life, just pray this simple prayer, and He will change your life.

Dear God, I know that I am a sinner. I know that you love me and want to save me. Jesus, I believe You are the Son of God, who died on the cross to pay for my sins, I believe God raised You from the dead, I now turn from my sin and, by faith, receive you into my life as my personal Lord and Savior. Come into my heart, forgive my sins, and save me, Lord Jesus. In your name I pray, Amen.

Lose Yourself, Pursue Jesus

Matthew 10:39 (NLT)

*"If you cling to your life, you will lose it;
but if you give up your life for me, you will
find it."*